In which music

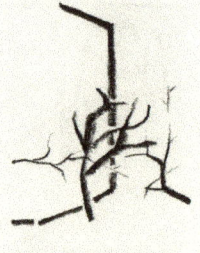 

is always folded within a fold — a representation of the enclosed world

In which music

Greg Darms

Radiolarian Press
Astoria / Northampton

Copyright 2018 by Greg Darms
All images © Greg Darms
All rights reserved

Radiolarian Press
Astoria, Oregon
Northampton, MA

First Edition

ISBN 978-1-887853-42-2

Contents

freshet
    Green ochre chrysalis   3
    Quietly   4
    And beyond   5
    Broken blue   6
    Distichs: Here is a darker time changing   7
    Gemini heart rock   8
    Freshet   9

nine assays
    River notes   13
    Drawings to things   14
    Thesis   15
    Wave section   16
    Ephemera   17
    Park tree   18
    Genesis   19
    Robert Ryman at DIA Chelsea   20
    The most desiring being   21

two tractates
    Spring ephemera   25
    Winter fragments   41

five essays
    Contorta   55
    from Raritan pages   59
    Spruce   63
    from Decalineal pages   67
    How paper   71

last year
    "breaking broken"   87
    "antiquarian case"   88
    "pod, berry, nut"   89
    "slowly ripening"   90
    "overwintered moss"   91

What if it were all just an overture and no one knew to what?
— Elias Canetti

1
freshet

Green ochre chrysalis

In this light
the daily not-yet seen.

Charged with belief,
aware of the charge.

Bright in, strange
out of context.

An invitation. Like any poem
taken both ways.

An expression for the thought,
a character for the word.

Ways of knowing
as if passing through.

Possible emergence
with wings, without wings.

Beautiful, and dangerous.
We know at least two things.

Breathing for silence
and space on the page.

Quietly

there has been and is — rain — grebe
the forest canopy — moves — my mind
the dark morning — natural entities
all day — thinking I — need something
many birds live — but none — seen
all night dreams — accumulative
one thing moving — and they — within
apposite — and original — to be found
arrival — here then — downstream wind
I can look myself up — in them — they
returning are always early — rippled
surface — fascicled — deep, desiring —

And beyond

the window, the world,
and through and beyond these things

(pressing my head against the glass
against the window screen, late,

and the first spring-in-winter gnat
on the other side "looking" in)

sitting here now then, as there,
waking, warming, arriving:

always arriving looking through,
sometimes having arrived and seen –

Broken blue

shell in the damp grass
above the tidal river

while the river's flood
is a sentry of silence

in the living morning
where all things are moving

from or toward being
hatched and whole or

cleft and split, unbound
and empty either way

Distichs: Here is a darker time changing

> *Or anywhere*
> *where stars blaze through clear air* (H.D.)

Third consecutive day of rain
That is no sky but a ceiling.

That is a sense of being placed
In place of darker left-hand chords.

Reflections here originate inside
The narrow room the only light lit.

The question of spring-or-not abused
Ten full days past the equinox.

What we have come to know as sky
Comes closer every day.

All night sky water on earth water
A grey-green noise below white.

Giving itself that way again and again
Receiving word of itself giving.

If this night of storm is strophe,
The epistrophe's the lesson: listen.

Ten thousand individual statements
Every second disattach.

This then the night of where we live
is close, illuminates.

Gemini heart rock

dark or light, dry or wet
on the beach, in the hand

a crooked vein of quartz
through the center

the path of our lives
to the love-joining

sandstone and slate
facing and touching each

other, the distance
between brought to zero.

Turn it over, the same.
We see us in this.

Freshet

of *atmos*, oxygen
surrounding waterwords
of sparrowsong, scatter
of finches in thunder.

Begin there. Tentative
at first, drops of rain
become sharp edge.

**2
nine assays**

River notes

A flight of geese first heard approaching from the west high over the wetlands heading toward the river, a great communal formal agreement reforming in each individual's instantaneous and timeless judgement of perception of the importance of this move toward actualization.

The sun rises at a point on the southeastern copse of spruce a fraction of a degree farther north, that is now for the first time in this new year in the hut-window pane, sending rays of light into my morning eye mind at the writing desk.

Today's intention is to read, and respond to, the world. The nominal rubric is the verb to be, in the sense of seeing and making. The inscription, finally: is.

Being on the water, you can look down to see up. There is no perfect correlation; you can read both ways. A western grebe swims floating on the surface between, eyes employed in both worlds.

Every thing is up to its own point involved in some future in its present becoming past, influenced by its own making and becoming the one choosing, chosen by experience.

The agentive experience of joy: the persistent vibratory achievement of intensive feeling that marks the interpenetration of individuals: the cross road between subjectivity and objectivity: how an actual entity becomes constitutes what the actual entity is.

Sixty-seven geese $[67 \times (1+0)] : [(\text{one seen once}) \text{ seen}] : [67^{67}/67^{67} = 1]$.

Thinking through this, the tree in its history is willing to let go to gravity, to weather, to spring sunlight and osmotic pressure, further binding or unbinding in its growth.

Late in the day I listen with hope and desire for birds gathering in flight, transiting the diminishing diurnal, circling lower and lower to light on stubble field or glassy slough. Nothing, that is expected. But closer, look. One song sparrow works the inch of edge containing the still bright lining of sky.

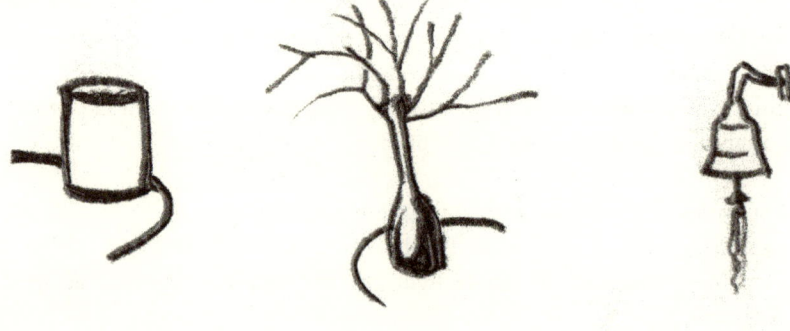

Drawings to things

The day took shape as a material structure of time.

The leaves had scattered and settled into place.

The page became a series of concentric spaces.

The text began to breed its own commentary.

The crows circled and arced in toward the hawk before spiralling away.

full-sun revery as if dreaming in the dark one kind of writing within another an intention toward attention sensed newly now edging one's own thinking to a grid or net to catch fragments in coherent punctuation the idea'd form of found nothings or lost findings many ways to some one thing, qualified nouns summoning

A thesis :

nouns doing not naming   improper, uncommon
not upper or lower case   transnominatively other
as far from chance as rain   registering incredulity
breaking up, turning down   peopleless, placeless,
thingless   in full self-possession
frost, leaf, merganser   the wren, the fungus, the fern
amanita, eel, kinnickinnick subject of, subject to things
obsession, box, abstraction   firstvisible form
deadhead sinksteel lagbolt   deepseeing subject to
its own revision   keeper of its own definition
solid, liquid, gas   concept open
to being opened   existing to open being again

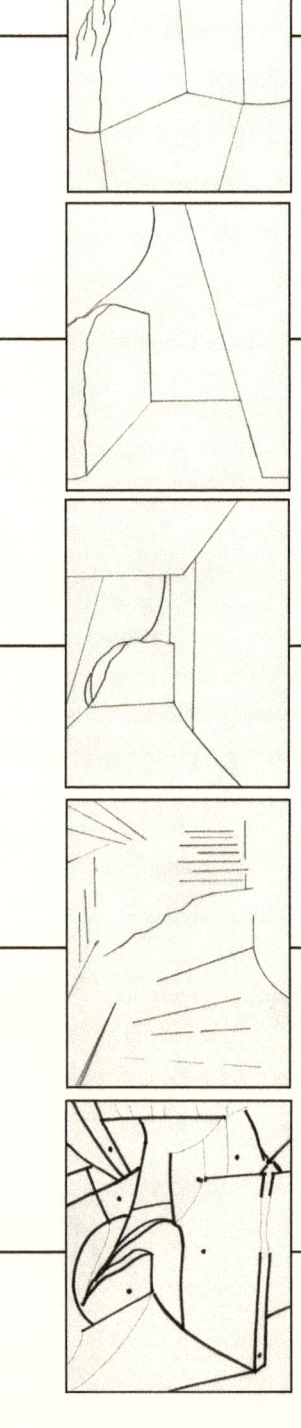

Wave section

drawing one hour one corner of the museum against boredom and certainty and futility toward some unknown inside more interior observationally felt form of formal, an experimental series of speculative linear enclosures and escapes from a cross-sectional perception of a model of a cross-section of a wave on display

kronokonstruktionskizzen
anima mundi linearis
an act which stirs the soul of time
study for the seal of the instant
the attitude that goes deeper than that
revolutionary subversion of material necessity

transformation of the impulse through connection and furthering of particular contrasts of intense experience in which the next actualization will be differently attributed instantaneously across time

cross-section of wave in a corner of the museum
a full hour in a / with a place
drawing lines of exile and collision
that any time can be a formative period
with the discovery of an inner compulsion

Ephemera

      a few words in a space for some purpose or for themselves
a page to be read a sheet to be sent a score to be sung a box to be opened
something to be   anything inasmuch as it is   its own minute
destination   close to, far from home

      the specific infinite   partial drawing of partial kallosphere
the seen a map for seeing   leaning into the darker ground cover shadow
noting the no thing the not yet   the theory and practice of hidden lines
catching the eye

      the sense of stopping in a given space   nowhere near zero
willing to come inside with indefinite forms   breaking the surface
the afterimage effect of language   elements of imagination spread out
and over a rolling concept

      we can see here a fragment which has become quiet   its entire
surface (its interior) never seen at once   in our day window of seeing
of making seeing thing   where lingering is allowed   small grounds
for a fine inscription

Park tree

Increase the contrast until every line itself stands and begins to walk, to run,

Fill in that line make it even more itself following express tracks, expressing

The infinite difference in miniscule gradations, like oak trunk against the sky

A drawing, a drawing fine, a bold figuration developing in the bath of ground

This me telling what it is to do, what form, what shape-taking intensity take

To press, impress on the page in question, open to interpretation and chance

Looking longingly through the flat photograph the starkly chiaroscuro trace

γενεση

The word for a thought a thing representing the agency of coming into being. The nearest approach to naming the nameless, to pinning the tag to origin. The surface hue and brilliancy of a long and ever darker string of connections. Earth's phenotype, *gaia phainein*, the visible phenomenon, thin opaque skin. The idea of gene, materialization of deep time, timelessness, back to black water. A string of, if not miracles, affinities in space, intimate and whelming attractions. Convoluted, involuted, in line with spirals and helices of fields of invisible force. Arrives, breaking through in splashing light, as if embodying morning in its

Genesis

Robert Ryman at DIA Chelsea

[suggested silence]

[wavy errors – distractions – welcome]

[wish for a place to sit – and not be in the gaze of guards]

[build square within confines of frame]

[all edges then erased]

[for effect of absence or absence of effect]

[the resistance to fullness or complete definition]

[what can be said about white nothing]

[from what distal or proximal thought of the form in the end of this]

[to draw white with white]

[to draw white without white]

[to write upon nothing]

[to drift away from words in the polyglot street]

[toward what]

[suggested silence]

The most desiring being

[a vegetal found-object textuality]

[a little drawing of process-passing]

[a one-word picture of the blank page]

[a singular character on vacation]

[a mirror-image of where the root is headed]

3
two tractates

Spring ephemera
— from the notebook of 2013

a new next first page — this internal pressure into the void — ah white!

nothing, much to write —

monitoring the long and the short waves — the static silences —
white noise in which music —

having reached a point, positionless — and the point in moving is?

[a line at a time — concatenate, incorporate — form as a step in the making]

the texture of a piece drawn from the canon, apocrypha, the body, the ground

each page a volume, volumes — each volume a page —

the ground, the grounding of the page — its materiality —

the copula of simple predication —

to make a pure mark, a mark of pure intention —

out of 'nothing' — nerves, muscle, energy —

pencil as brush —

words as
words for
words to
words of

correct beginning
illuminated speculum
illustrated exemplar
precious mirror
vernacular translation
collectanea of the Shoushan Pavilion
comprehensive list
diary of transcribing
one hundred selections from The Five Classics
dream of nine clouds
album of the song Thinking of Beauties
record compiled in idleness
complete collection of the inner quarters

after what-it-is-seen-as, given-a-namebefore —

[the dialectic
implied by the
sudden blank
space]

                                        numbernought
                                        imagempty
                                        nothingword
                                        suddenstart
                                        spacecapacity

> a given number, unknown quality
>
> uncertain origination, ordination
>
> key concept, loosely articulated
>
> vagrant center, respectable aura
>
> tight structure, void of meaning

great form is shapeless –
how write how
not be exposed

negative counter-negative sententiae

Know the white.
Keep to the black.

[live in no certain order]

Ponder page (rock, cliff wall) fulfillment.
Think mountains and clouds uninscribed.

> uninscribed
>
> but there is no brush that big

Limn the prolegomena to an eventual exegesis.

(ritual meaning of textual form)

Individual verses and phrases of the Shijing functioned like a kind of grand vocabulary.

further seeing as   a "transformation text"
is line written —

when *is*
a word —

is *when* is
not so verbal —

synonymic
states of residence —

lyric manifest
in text box —

[a container of
origins]

in the absence of
history, commentary

words on walls
here inscribed

write on white
something to read

leaded glass	reconstructed shards	spider web in amber
vagrant letterforms	pendant stalk	stamp album
retinal arc weld	lost polygons	relief rubbing
box section	string wrap	melismatic lineation
untranslation	lost meaning found	metaphysicality
protracted square	rereticulation	brain scan

... words in breath, earth in time ...

to have a place to go to be to give –

words, and then thoughts of images (writing, to be seen –

starting (tending, inclining) to see while writing –

incipient desire to put it in (as) glyphs –

> ... the eye lets us see what it hears, tastes,
> touches. In my body, I am all eyes. – Jabès

[with the mark, an influx of lexicality]

stasis – storm warning
static – good walk
imminent – immanent
just sitting by window
fresh spring – green tea
column of figures
page of characters
chisel-style – brush
stylus – Point made
word for grey-green
mark – meaningful
stichic – line up for
long lining – point
far north and true

fading reticulations
instantaneous succulents
slow snake seeking
partially surrounded by infinities
cumulus
thingly association
what being there engenders

walking stirs the ground
at the limit of appearing
embedded forms emerge
still everything moves
keep the book open in the hand
moving on, remembering
brushwillow, bramblebud
naming it living

writing with a limited lexicon

symbol, sign for alchemical process

solid form empty receptacle

one in one, zero in zero

instant negative script

[placement: momentary dwelling]

addendum et subtractum

kingfisher poise: position

focus where the world stops

photograph/umbragraph : thought/mind

having been found having (finding)

drawing what I will, willing

limit ever changing

opening the crucible

< Resistance arises wherever we would go,
and movement arises wherever we would stop. >

•

dream – involving words, writing, page, book, art, life, work – making words (characters, marks) on pages – each unique, each uniquely 'correct' in its own manifestation – beyond meaning, judgement, value, yet coinciding with all – it feels like revelation, the 'perfection' of each present and successive work/ expression, the total acceptance of who and what I am and what I do –

•

what is the reciprocal of a word?

•

after forgetting, forge

•

100% clear sky, we head out early to walk the beach at Seaside, find patches of baby sand dollars, sit in warm sun against a log near the dune-grass –

[a word for this]

•

overlapping origins

compound possibility

•

(   ) when (what) it (was)

word
        (write it now or
                      (almost enough)

implied passage
vertical presence
descending moments

                        [gloss on the previous
                        the concurrent
                        maybe to be –

                        in which any
                        as well as every
                        passes through]

the river low – little rain or snowmelt – willows fuzzy light green – cottonwood air

binomial construction

parallel construction

seal / grid

cosmological template

white/pink manzanita flowers, pink-to-white
greasewood greening under thorns

cascades of Deschutes
big ponderosa-lava, pine wind

10,000 pine-twig segments,
fallen-broken writing –

ephemeral spider blown down to page
from the windy canopy –

a close look at earth
from this kneeling prospect —

hint of the infinite: stylistic variations
inherent in the 'three-needle' form —

. . . but it's the emptiness . . .
What lights up the world is the mind.

from nothing, only something
from dark, light

[a compilation of erasures]
page after page of incipits—of singularities —
every page a template, from a template —

written words are fallen (landed) spiders —
blow-down script —

ground : ground litter :: text : medium
as below, so below below —
found ground — scattered runelike parascript
                                        implying such as
rimrock blocks, river erratics, microfault lines, patterns of flow and standing
waves, lichen encrustations, basalt exfoliations, tracks in mud, splash-line,
algae-band —

                     cliff and talus read like trigrams in place —
                     varieties of bifurcation —

the glyph
the day's first word

looking to refind, found —

opening   the near book
                   always apposite

          remember   understand   wake up

[begin]

白赤黒青黄緑紅紫紺朱

with what is near

empty   dark   potential

not more and more

white
red
black
green-blue
plants by moonlight
yellow
green
crimson
purple, violet
dark blue
vermilion

if no reading no writing –
a reconstructed wartime-baroque-organ concept

like a new edition of apocrypha
infinitely hard to find

a skip during the epiphany –
during which someone died –

in the shadow of its shadow,
of having not, not having

the benefit or curse of news
of not making something of it –

so it is, and may not be
a case of conditional syllogistics –

•

horsetail & fiddleneck thrust –
dazzling white sky packages –
surges & reversals – yin yang and back –
calm sun, cold wind, contained in each other –
shared transgressions, winter-in-spring –
to draw a metaphysical swirl, or swerve –
the truth of it on my skin –
period of duration and period of full stop –

[a number of first pages, each page a reciprocal relation of decision and chance]
$$until\ x=x$$
(while, during, since)

function words of indeterminacy – indeterminate functions of words –

changeable syntax – function of word function of position –

graphic language in flux –

this far into it, before settling on *a* or *the* –

ideas passing moments words light –

eleven elevations, concentrated concepts –

book-open toy-flag chemical-flash –

words for the sake of all sentient beings –

    be yourself a child of words

: a temporary (temporal) network of concordances

first red of rhododendron – pink camellias fill – reddish-blue vinca – animal flare-ups, sparrow, hummingbird, squirrel – sporadic sun – sitting on the hut deck late afternoon with pot of Soaring Crane tea, thinking (sparrow song) – not of words-for, not of words-arising-and-passing – no name –

new templates

old forms new words, old words new forms

older than time, newer than time

[write my own language]

what knowledge not why the world   (first goldfinch

just how it feels being having losing

gaining just this in the interim
this easy nameless everything

        content with weather
        reading the body
        sitting more often
        sitting longer longer
        warmed by two suns
        full belly full
        floating on the river
        not moving much
        green black forest
        small silver fish
        plenty of light
        vision good enough
        living today living
        twenty-five thousand days

                                          (one mallard mid-river

[old script new brush; new script old brush; new script new brush]

into the deep dark, to run down and collect there, sea, playa, belly –

written here for the first time – nova scriptum, scriptio, scriptura –

ANNOTATED TALKS ON STONES
THE TEXTUALIZED MOUNTAIN
THE ENMOUNTAINED TEXT
INSCRIPTION FOR A RITUAL FIELD
RECORD OF PAINTING CLOUD MOUNTAIN
INQUIRY INTO METAL AND STONE
INVESTIGATIONS OF FOUR MOUNTAINS

gesture in art and criticism – art of critical gesture –

critique in gestural art – verbal expression as the art of the possible –

landscapes of poetic ideas – leaves of paintings and leaves of calligraphy

transcriptions of many inscriptions –

importance as a unique object –

entering the mountain is not avoiding the world –

all things are as they are by virtue of themselves –

[translinguistic lexicon, commonplace book of ideograms]

any *one* and its *many* – numerical antonymity – exigetical mirror –

no question this is unknown –

•

A regime of sun is installed, with golden crowns, red wings, and still-water reflections sky of earth and earth of sky – flight and flow, bright and grow, higher senses of springing from the mud, nests under eaves again, among new leaves again a calmer clearer urgency.

That I can and do come back to words, my gift received and given, eyes opening to ancient sounds.

That sitting on the surface here is ground for superscripts of swallow cursive epigraphs of heart.

morning nest on the south sun porch
not-forcing following listening

making of not-making
momentary things

survived travels and transits
arrived nowhere in no time

the state of violet-green free-soaring
(swooping) language setting itself free

in the state of being born, changing
form, being born

and being born, being changing
not just something you see you think

from nowhere somewhere behind below
inscribing with a very light hand

         writing as a way of being

         a result of listening

         a naming and making visible

[every line, every page a dedication]

Winter fragments

first

1   Before beginning the road, the way of always beginning.

2   As if nothing outside of inward-reflecting window, face to glass, distant star-like suggestions of sudden flaring appearances, swallowed again. As in Hindemith's *Trauermusik* – the dark lit, maybe. This access to and transit of thought and language for springing free and all.

3   Dead serious weather, formless news – without photograph, maybe a text – without text, maybe a memory.

4   Formal identity of communal aspens near the great divide – immersion in original text, transcription of realia.

5   The Library – annal of forgotten events, concordance of archaic words, card catalog of Babel, facade of mirrors, seminary of stone. One can wear the nexus down to a nub, to a perfectly clear window.

6   The Museum – follow the "Big Bang" directional arrow through dioramas of plastered overgrowth to the "Hall of the Universe."

7   Most of the transcript for these days is elsewhere.

8   Mapless and lost in The Village, aware of the anaphora and concatenation in this sequence of participles, consulting the oracle in passing surfaces, gathering, condensing, writing the way out.

9   An eye awake upon any of this becomes lit.

second

1   Thinking about opening the time-remaining door.

2   Reading deep in that time.

3   Only every possible inflection, turn of thought: small-frame drawings of skylines, horizon-lines, and architecture.

4   Jade (from name of Mountain) from mountain.

5   Glyph graven into wrought ground – into, on, and underneath the surface.

6   Shadows, tendrils, mycorrhyzae – so-called abstract expressions. Loss forever accepted.

7   In "slow glass" – angle of incidence, of reflection – one's own reading.

8   Loose correspondence – with things as they stand. Nothing speaking to nothing.

9   The last note finely drawn – out – becomes itself, in a new light.

third

1   A song cycle in a strange language – new; other. So a different attention is called for.

2   Which line in a text is melody. Which is continuo, which is descant. Which line in a composition is text.

3   One added to ten thousand is one hundredth of a percent: .00001

4   Winter begins with rain. Some words-that-mean are life-giving, give life to language.

5   Condense like starlings into a field, or disperse like siskins into the sky. Every ground retains a trace of recent intentions.

6   Ideas rising from monochrome fields. Expressions of mute impressions. Drawings of rain at night. How to focus on indeterminacy. Everything permeable and permeated.

7   Gestural traces, genetic restatements, palimpsests of ephemera. White on white. Songs after Ryman, line drawings after Ligeti.

8   A series of cyclonic disturbances from the far northwest, from The Gulf of Alaska – rain after rain. What finite number of instantaneous elemental embraces, or bridges spanning or connecting what durations in the storm, exist, or are implied.

9   When rain is just rain, raindrops are only raindrops and water is itself, water.

10   Every thing that belongs to time is between, is broken, is parenthesis, is a line between line breaks, is an interval in the containment of itself.

fourth

1   What we know by now of such near misses – little by little and bit by bit – obligato repetons – is in dancing with lines, in drawing the current.

2   See, say – then saw, seen – then said.

3   Here. Hear here – kind of thing.

4   What (we might know) can begin to be said in C Major. An image. A word. A catchy tune. And in C# Minor?

5   Of what importance, the first five rewrites of a poem about a frail sculpture of a vessel for the passage of time.

6   Each variation a new theme: variation of themes = theme of variations.

7   All are, all is.

8   Attempts at straight lines and perfect arcs – themeless variations with supposedly real consequences. The potential of structure released by gesture.

9   The reaching for and the finding – simultaneous expressions of the one and the many, the self and the other.

10   On shelves in the Library of Intensity, pages containing nested inscriptions of written drawings of variations of light.

fifth

1   Folk music – people singing. What is heard is something below the sound. A dissonance, incorporated – solitary loon call.

2   Out of time, before everything forever at the end – heard.

3   This. It. Now. Here. "Tzu."

4   In shorter days, longer intervals. Approach and departure of a plurality of singularities.

5   Stretch a word, a silence. Make room for intuition, chance, risk, accident.

6   Everything – anything along or within sight of these lines – left behind as drawn.

7   Before it is remembered – the open field.

8   The whole look of the page and the breath of the text.

sixth

1   The particular universal parallel couplet.

>   Full moon flood tide.
>   Dazzling cold winter light.

2   What is pictured forever is here now, is a question, remaining.

3   What will, become fragment. Piece, together. Calm and clear in its own form.

4   With application of pressure to stylus, and of ink to memory – sung on the edge of lyric.

5   A drawing of a performance of a lyric of a poem of Celan set to music by Kancheli – like all momentarily contiguous durations, equally impossibly infinitely perfect.

6   The tendency of music to create its own text. Text its own reading. Image. Sound.

7   A book of compressed specimens: a purposeful fragmentary. Some sensibility in variora.

8   A book of new and collected seals. Every vehicle carries its own temporality, caught in its own matrix.

9   A poem inscribed on a wall – a thinking line – draws attention through gesture and contour of both language and material.

10   Text block – intratextual gloss – illumination – marginalia. Rubrics of figure and ground, intention and possibility.

seventh

1   Thinking of clearing thought. The idea of a new idea.

2   In the space between experience and meaning, with the latest (last) falling leaves – building a catalog of empty (open) subjects.

3   Thymus, spleen, gut-mind: between inner and outer, bring all the chemistry together.

4   Ready to receive – image of permeability, active transport across membranes, windows that open, doors. Skylight, earthlight.

5   Art: staying open (changing-with) – being in the open – of the becoming.

6   What word for it at this time (non-Cartesian desire).

7   To unwrap the condition of nestedness – make available nodes, tender surfaces – sublimate precious square-inches – unbury and illuminate shadowy complexes.

8   What word then for this first.

9   The kind of thought that circles squares – the word the square, the word the circle.

10   The words of condition themselves unwrapped.

eighth

1   Renewal. Morning-day of dwelling as change-and-return. Opening the hut.

2   Feel the stitch-binding in the neck and living in the world hold, release, and dissolve.

3   Reading it again for the first time – as if never – as if always. Jamais et jamais.

4   As 'reading falls under the heading of writing' – listen for, and to, the homegrown music.

5   Com-positionally, con-structively, dis-con-tinually, re-flectively, trans-formatively – enact, embody a form of thinking.

6   Transformational influences transformed. Nonindexical incipits indexed. Momentum of intellectual photons.

7   Ten seconds: winter: Northwest coast: black and yellow passage: Townsend's warbler.

8   All finches, juncoes, and sparrows vanish: sharp-shinned hawk: morning dockside river green: a few leaves fall from the sky.

9   Grey-white under-cumulus reflections on south faces of south-wind-rising wavelets; on all ever-other sides, the north-slope wave-shadows complete the complement, the weave. Full-sun breakthroughs bring white highlights to the cloth.

10   One. One. Different in itself, unlike. One.

ninth

1   Cloud descends and rests on earth – pieces of sky and sky are one – yet $1 > 0 \;;\; 1 < 2$.

2   The ground shows through everywhere – a recitative loop, a polyvocal ostinato.

3   Can everything be caught in this narrow spectrum of mute wet light.

4   How did the rain fall before words.

5   Contained – light, or dark – its limits – so the possible opening.

6   Reread – reconstruct – still be the first time.

7   Cloud resumes status as ceiling in clear sky as night falls, and all is interiorized. The day-ending time of the world begins. Winter day can fit into summer night.

8   Sky, cloud, earth, night are one. $1 + 1 + 1 + 1 = 1$. And $= 0$, and/or zero. Nothing partial if nothing fully seen.

9   Origin of poem on its night page.

10   The day is saturated with eternally available color sounds.

tenth

1   One among many is one – its breaths, its receding steps, its fading echoes.

2   Time and place – moving the state of being into the next frame. A curious relationship between the serial and the unique.

3   No one-to-one correspondence – finding self in next likely place of saying so.

4   Under the heaven-threaded person-hood, the eye open.

5   Title, index, concordances after the fact – of some one at the center of the circle of vision.

6   The legendary Box X found at the bottom, brought back to light, placed in the tokonoma, opened in the company of family and friends. Apparently empty, a receptacle for words.

7   What if we could not remember, had no memory. Can a thought be born and can it survive the instant sans duration. What language could exist only in a present.

8   No recognition without cognition. Even so, given mind enough and time, how much goes unnoticed and unsaid.

9   Many is the one among many. I would like to draw this one near.

10 Open further the eye in the hand, and the hand in the eye.

eleventh

1   To plan the arrival of a surprise – the birthday new year boy opens the door and yells, "!"

2   An opening celebration, invitation ouverte au monde. Se devenir, commencer à être.

3   Slow lead-in (B-flat minor adagio, Beethoven Symphony No. 4) to a series of joyous initiatory dedications. Then breaking through quietudes, "Here's to Astoria! Here's to New York! Hear! Hear! – to here!"

4   Past present. Past and present participles. Past always beginning. Now, if unknowable, present perceptible. As phenomenon, -ing, -ing. And existentially, -s, -s.

5   Then we heard everything singing in contrasts – a satisfying disharmony.

6   All, that is, are implicated in this performance. Side by side, each recognizable.

7   We. Oui. I. Eye. Aye.

8   A select constellation of 1000 characters, a boxed set of kindred inscriptions, a transcript constructed from the knit nest of singular pentimenti.

4
five essays

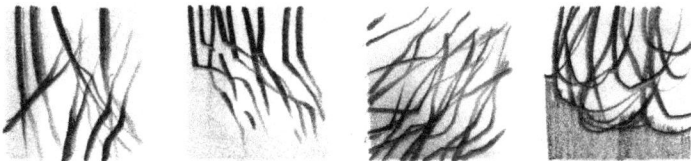

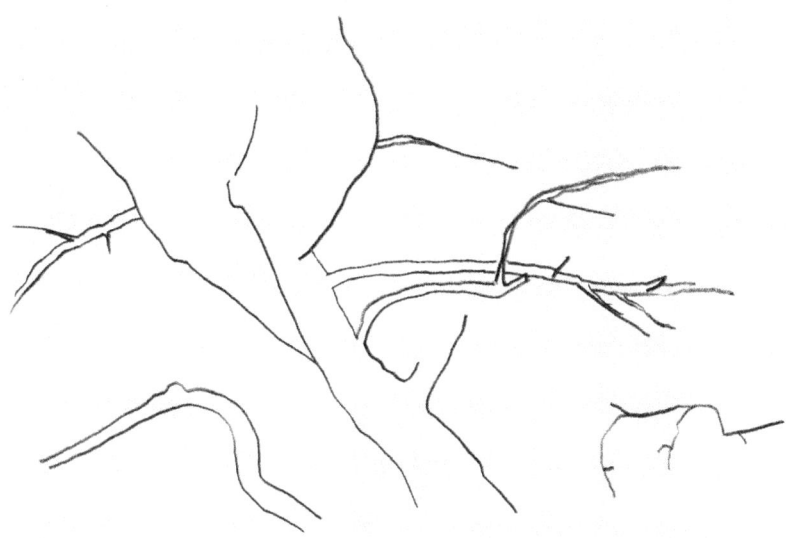

Contorta

1. There is no guide to the imminent ephemera.

2. Nature will not stop.

3. Reality is singularly momentous, a momentum of syntax.

4. It is often a matter of scale.

5. There is no definitive grammar.

6. There is only a trace of words in place.

7. Yet a fallen form, now visible, is a stopping point.

8. There is a serial nature inside itself.

1. In the ground, one of everything is possible.

2. Self-insufficiency engenders.

3. Soon a sentence forms.

4. Difference materializes.

5. Pages are connected by a line.

6. Aphorisms are flung into the world.

7. The number becomes numberless.

8. In just that idea is everything or nothing.

9. The extent to which this is possible is one living life.

10. The whole thing is involved.

1. A temporary subjunctive is not false.

2. A suspended identity of form may inspire a will to further synthesis.

3. One may be chosen by the materials in hand, whether they have been chosen or received as a gift.

4. Texts and pretexts suggext contexts.

5. The nature of a blank page is in its silence.

6. The nature of all other pages is in their variora.

7. Nature, the very world, the real thing – the osprey circling – is duration.

8. *Duration is ongoing genesis.*

from **Raritan pages**

1:1   What observable phenomenon can carry the twin cargoes of finite particularity and universal importance? How are these reconciled in the context of the moment, in the context of the continuum? What craft of attention can be brought to this encounter in order for the inherent intensities to be realized?

1:2   In a radical flattening, a planar compression to two dimensions, extensive low clouds have simultaneously brought the sky-ground forward to the surface and sent the forest-and-river-scape back to adhere to that surface. Now the window hangs on the wall like Josef Albers' nearly white on white print of the square.

1:3   As the afternoon light decreases lumen by lumen, art and reality stir slightly, seemingly affected by several formal ideas including montage and chiaroscuro. En scène, a grebe and a merganser are focal points – possibly key characters – before first one, then the other disappear below the surface.

2:1   Traveling by going no place, or by not-going in place. Meaning nothing more than everything that can be seen, as well as everything else, as it is felt, as it is desired. Meaning nothing less than the (even if, especially because) momentary perfection of each epistemically partial but phenomenally whole detail.

2:2   Silver-blue and green-black surface flicker, shimmer, time-textured dazzle of reflection and refraction. The winter's morning habitat for this year's resident divers, ever reenacting a skit of disappearance and representation. How many scenes in one act? How many plays within a play?

2:3   From this same vantage point, with this same parallax, toward this same set of vanishing points — this window, these two eyes — chariot-bound for seeing in universal coach-class, the always microcosmic horizon extends and renews itself at the river's proximal edge with as much disclosure as at the westward curve of the sea.

3:1   What meaning can be attached to photons, what importance to the general effect of light beyond its absolute specificity of illumination? Is every pointed ray of seeking intent on nothing but its own infinitely random agency? Is there nothing like attachment or importance outside of every one thing seen?

3:2   Only if and when an eye is open on a struck thing can seeing be. Wintering water birds work the barely visible, the rich, rewarding depth. Food is taken from the obscurity behind the mirror, with clarity of intent and definition. Grebe is satisfied with fish, then looks around with new eyes again.

3:3   Questions stand outside Aristotle's porch. Only in contexts of startle and wonder is a lyre struck. Invention of plectrum, and the sapphic stanza. Gull strikes eagle, and the world sings "I" from the wings. "You" are left to entertain notions of tragedy, genesis, and time in the sunlight, in the starlight, in the footlights.

4:1   Twenty thousand days lived to date are no proscription for living fully in this present. That there is only this one, and then this one. Everything has seen in every thing that part of each in each, that coeval duration if not named and honored, known the way rain knows the sea and sky, having felt contingency.

4:2   Assemblages in flux, in continual changes of state, coming together and falling apart. Nothing new in this thought: everything is always 'new'. The memory and recalled image of a single teenage sneaker step on a particular sidewalk in Berkeley in 1961 – every atom of concrete, every brain cell, having since moved on.

4:3   No question is ever necessary, and no answer is ever the last word. But each is contained in the other, a construction of mind in the discontinuum of matter, that is to say language, inscribe it. The latest gesture is the momentarily definitive, infinitive, what-can-be-affirmed-as-lasting in the hurdy-gurdy drone of time.

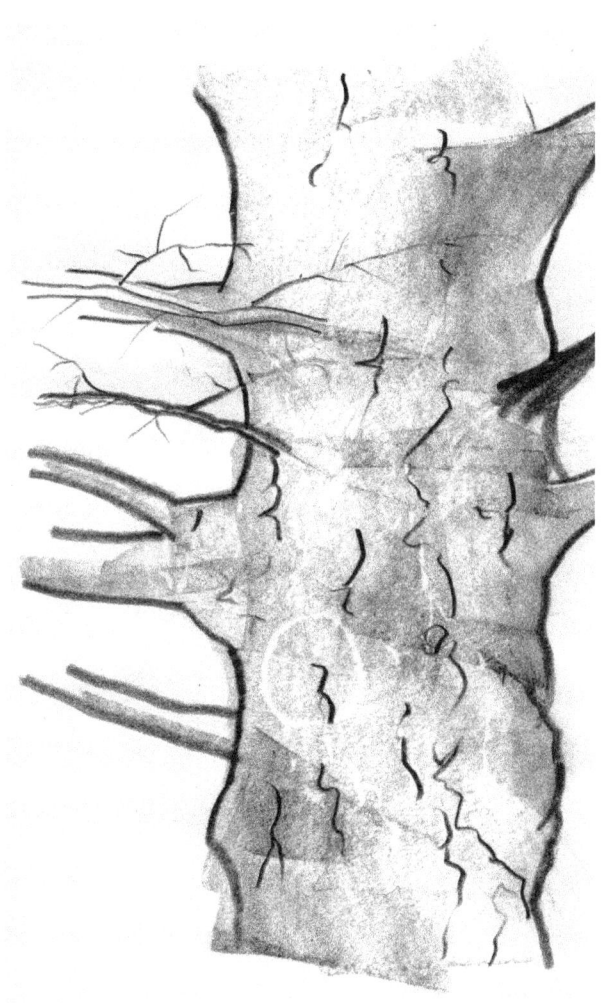

Spruce

trunk lines
bark lines
branch and twig lines
always thought lines
all lines broken
healing with green

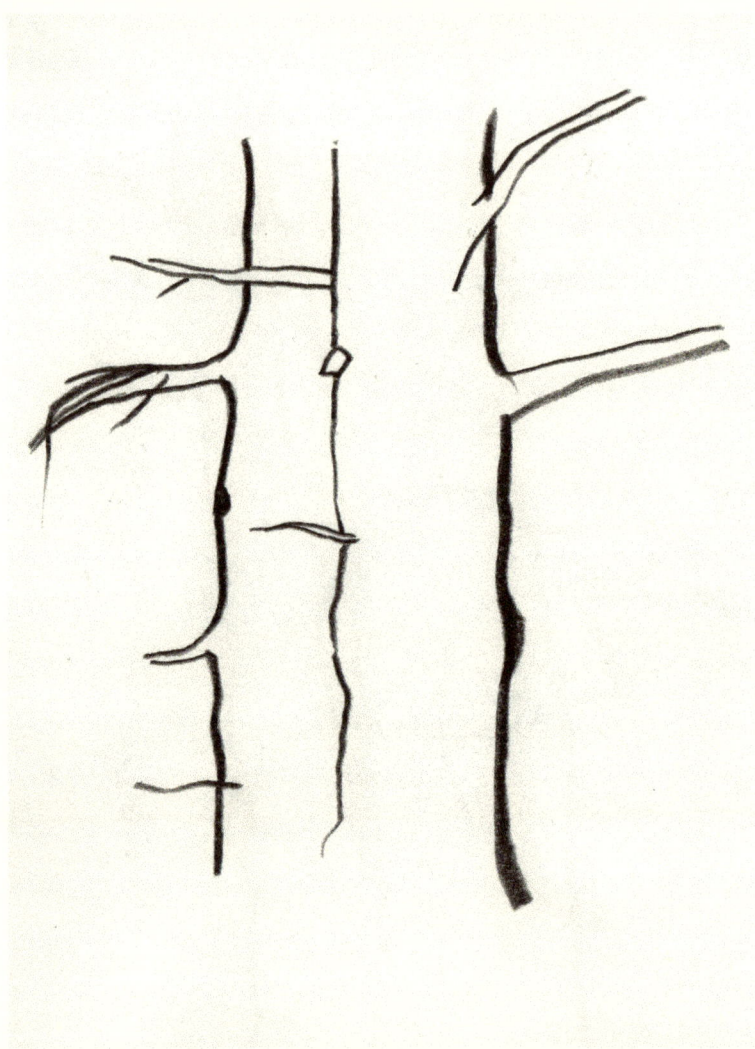

a book made of filled lacunae
positioned and appositioned segments
lit letters, unconditioned words,
bound signatures

external & internal structures
built in, built out
linear suggestions
glimpses, records
what you see & don't
see through both ways

from **Decalineal pages**

> *I only wish them to settle on a flower till I can come up with them to examine the powderd colours on their wings and then they may flutter off from fancy'd danger and welcom* — John Clare

1

with no mouth, with love and the soul, with
stardust – with innocence and experience, with
a thinking eye, with forms of ruin – with
the marks in the fields, open secrets
of beauty – archives, stones – gloom and
glory – open to thoughts and words
things and events – dreaming of desert
hot springs, wild horses, waterfall ferns
feeling being in the middle of – beginnings
endings – with paper and pencil –

2

lots of little different things – significant
figures of alterity – space for chemistry
between appositional bodies – or gestures
waving at or away from – each – other –
sentient figures imagined into existence –
books in the library – words in the book –
nuance upon variation – delicate lava-
flow shadings of interiority – I did
today in deep time – dreaming geologic-
ally – feed the cats – stretch – a poem

3

shades of quiet – plural – drawing
breath from nothing, nothing from
daily light, nightly dark – as cycle of re-
invention, re-formation – lying fallow – inter-
mezzic, between the furrows – analog as respite
from digital – cessation as relief from in-
cessance – the non-arising twenty-four scaup
floating out of range, below radar –
not wrong, as silence is not in the field
of dialectics – as nothing gives over to every –

4

contemporaneous origins – multiple
as words in the world, things in duration
language an event or continuum of pauses
instantaneous exposures overlapping
at once everything including the absent
and only this one once: and – a view
of intersecting sententiae – make of
it, if any thing, less of a system, or not
necessarily more of necessities – looking out
for, on the high flood-tide – slightest proof –

5

waiting above sleep for nothing known –
clock tick – a motor on then off in the world –
lineless time in an imaginal space – wake
to sense irreality – difference in the home –
place of writing backwards in a night mirror –
is everyword metamorphed here – is question
to answer – old blanket around shoulders –
in this hour this atmosphere prayer – tides
swell below & beneath the house – leaving
beings exposed – later to cover them again –

6

tinge in left ring finger – a shoulder click –
reminder to remember – live between flex
and extend – preposition as proposition –
finding form or a rock – the rising thought–
what if each of these books – were I rock
enough to see it that way – its posture mine
learning the way it reminds itself – still,
counting nothing – zero, zero, zero – until
no until – just written and read like a text –
were feelings, say – or butterflies –

How paper

from the wild in the wind here who knows where or when but there uncultivated without definition inside the outer mind no rule book ever written conceived even but without value yet must catch crystallize or purify bring to paper how

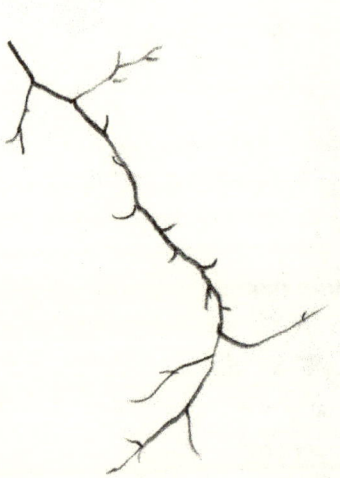

branches, veins,

and thought

an eye awake upon any of this becomes lit

which thing comes close

is waiting there

backlit, suspended

that it may be the partial, the ephemeral, the first-time, the present, the passing, the felt, the strong, the invocative, the had-to-be-there, the is and was

                        intensity

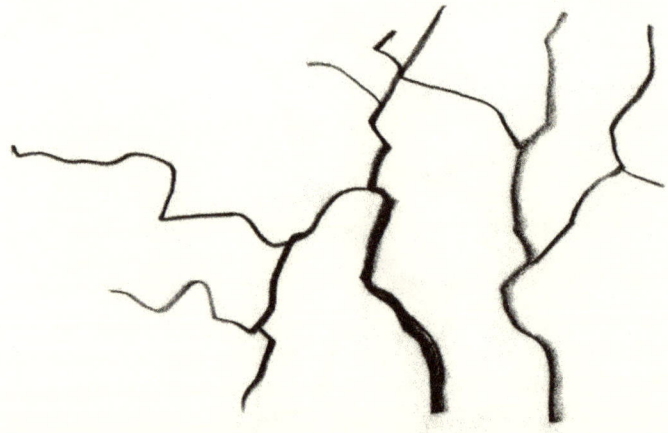

savannah sparrow in willow-thicket – seen from within the thicket – so both seen

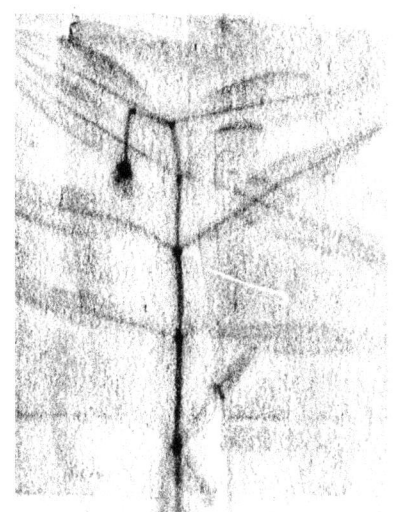

partially not

entirely is

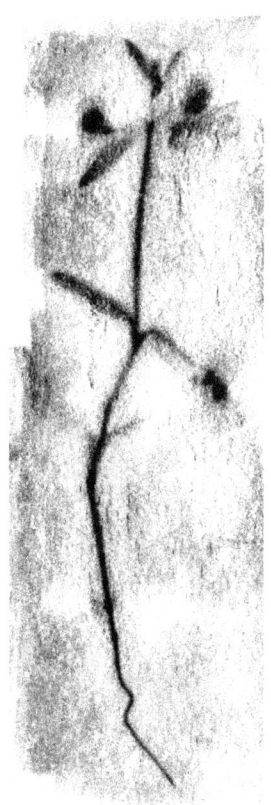

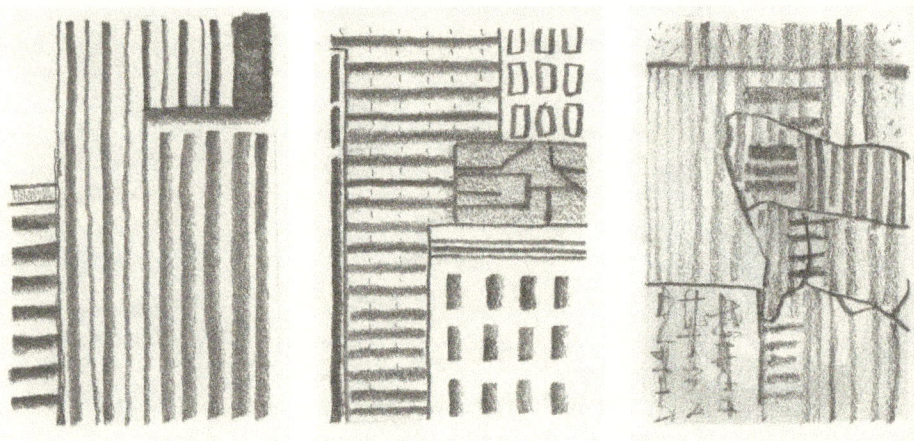

a totality that is exceeded where words become things
the code no longer suffices – the translation is infinite

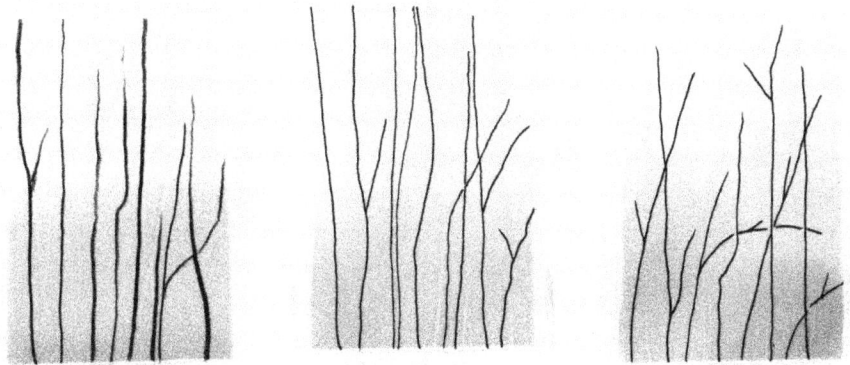

just words as facts, the matter of this now rising in the empty field like weeds

  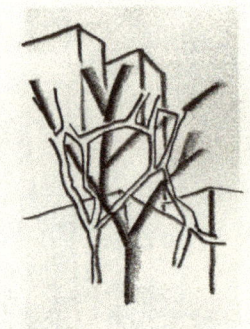

a word or phrase not dependent on transcendence, able and willing to stand side by side with itself if necessary or momentarily full of worldly meaning in no time flat – as long as it takes – at the intersection of 88th and Lexington

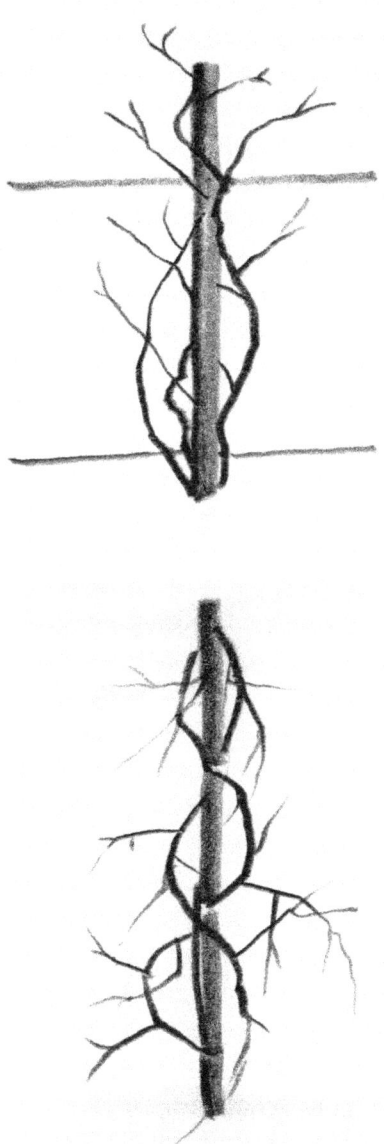

a reflection on things being wrapped in words, words on beings reflected in things wrapped in themselves, themselves being thoughts on the things nominally verbalized de- and re-constructed, wrapped and unwrapped, marginalized and made whole anew as things on paper, material in mind, forms inflected by the positive space made available in the real world

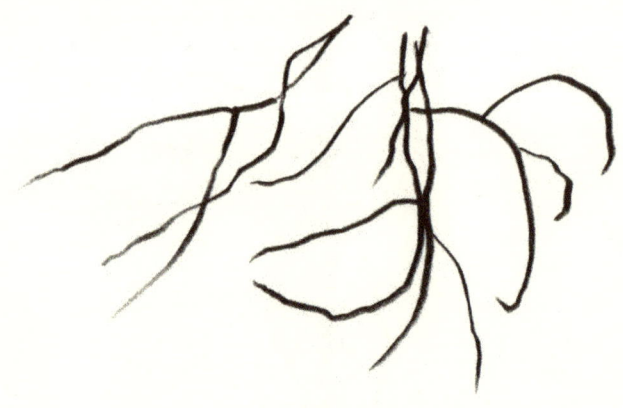

[[nested] language]

the basis of thought

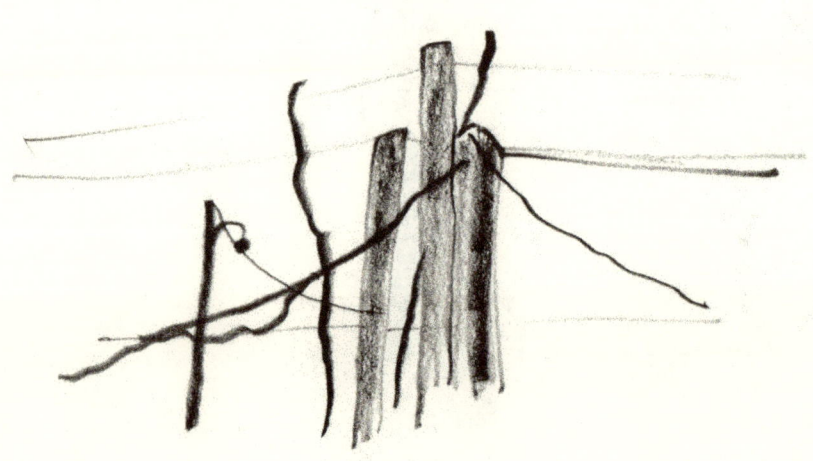

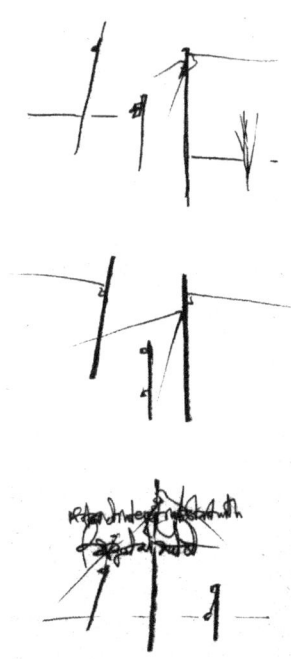

each window
opening on other
windows opening

5
last year

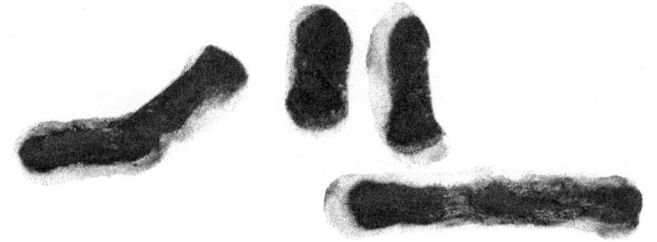

breaking broken
structure remains
to Spiraea attached
brittle wood form
near to return
still of last year

antiquarian case empty now
of green cells, ovule, seed
yet a dry stigma describes
a descending arc, french-curved
cooly darkly reddish wood
the Rhododendron memories
of last year hardened to cellulose
'deadhead' still alive to light

pod, berry, nut over-wintered
become tenuously mobile art
internal thoughts of fertile seed
become clustered paradigm
what's left of what's left of
what was—is there no time
for inconsequential flowers?
for preserves of memorial fruit?

slowly ripening
just beginning to
fill its own form
letting go its ties
to world origins
names for parts
fall into the past
leave little scars
opposite the now
significant stem
newly attached
sense of exterior
secret plenitude
for late summer

overwintered moss
never finished as in 'done for'
fruiting at the tip
keeping its interest alive
possibly unfathomable
in definitive terms
dancing with closure
& disclosure
surface of infinite series of
jumping-off points
with feelings so near the
surface

This book was designed by the author in the waning days of far west wet-winter work. **In which music is** now seen as the third volume in an Astorian "Floating Hut Trilogy," preceded by **Flammable, Inflammable** in 2007, and **Para,Taxis** in 2011. Typeface is Joanna, with Frutiger titles.

www.ingramcontent.com/pod-product-compliance
Lightning Source LLC
Chambersburg PA
CBHW031202090426
42736CB00009B/764